Read & Respond

Ages 7–11

Read & Respond

Ages 7–11

Author: Jillian Powell

Editor: Tracy Kewley

Assistant Editor: Niamh O'Carroll

Series Designer: Anna Oliwa

Designer: Liz Gilbert

Cover Image: Dan Krall

Illustrations: Martin Salisbury and Mike Phillips/Beehive Illustration

Text © 2010 Jillian Powell © 2010 Scholastic Ltd

Designed using Adobe InDesign

Published by Scholastic Ltd, Book End,
Range Road, Witney,
Oxfordshire OX29 0YD
www.scholastic.co.uk

Printed by Bell & Bain

1 2 3 4 5 6 7 8 9   0 1 2 3 4 5 6 7 8 9

British Library Cataloguing-in-Publication Data
A catalogue record for this book is available from the British Library.

ISBN 978-1407-11897-0

Acknowledgements

The publishers gratefully acknowledge permission to reproduce the following copyright material: **Faber & Faber Ltd** for the use of the cover of *The Midnight Fox* by Betsy Byars (2006, Faber & Faber).
Viking Penguin A division of Penguin Young Readers Group, A member of Penguin Group (USA) Inc for the use of extracts from *The Midnight Fox* by Betsy Byars. © 1968, Betsy Byars.
Every effort has been made to trace copyright holders for the works reproduced in this book, and the publishers apologise for any inadvertent omissions.

The Midnight Fox

About the book

Betsy Byars has said that *The Midnight Fox* is probably her own favourite of the books she has written, and the first that 'turned out the way (she) had hoped it would'. Like many of her novels, the story draws strongly on personal experience and memory. It is the first into which she introduced autobiographical elements, like the newspaper headlines she and her sister Nancy used to conjure up when they were children, and the doll's head, which the dog brought home, that kept popping up in unexpected places. She has said that in this way her novels are like 'scrapbooks of her life', bringing back memories. Betsy has been fascinated with wild animals since she was a child, and wanted to work with them when she grew up. A wild fox is one of several animal themes – other novels feature swans, a wounded crane, horses and dogs.

First published in 1970, the novel is narrated in the voice of Tom, a sensitive boy whose lack of athletic prowess is, he is convinced, a disappointment to his parents. Tom's world revolves around model making and hanging out with his best friend Petie. He can't swim or run fast, and is afraid of lots of things, including animals. When his parents take a cycling holiday in Europe, Tom is sent to stay with his aunt and uncle on their farm, a prospect he dreads. But gradually, he begins to unwind and open up to his surroundings and his world is transformed by the unexpected sighting of a rare and beautiful black fox and her cub. When the fox steals the farm's turkey, his uncle decides to hunt her down and Tom has to overcome his diffidence and find a way to save the vulnerable fox family. It is a story about the magic and transforming power that wildlife can bring to our lives. Tom is taken out of his comfort zone and comes face to face with living creatures and real issues – a world away from the model making and play-acting of his humdrum home life.

About the author

The American author Betsy Byars was born in North Carolina in 1928. Her father worked as a bookkeeper in a cotton mill, and Betsy and her elder sister Nancy went to school in a cotton-mill village. As a child, Betsy loved reading and at college she changed courses from maths to English. In 1950 she married Ed Byars, a lecturer and pilot, and they moved to Illinois. With four young children, Betsy began writing articles for newspapers and magazines. She loved reading to the children and began writing stories for them, having her first story, *Clementine,* published in 1962. Betsy and her husband, both licensed pilots, live on an airstrip in South Carolina with a hangar for their planes built under the house and the studio where Betsy writes on the top floor. Betsy has written more than 60 stories for children and young people. Her novels have been translated into 19 languages and won awards including the Newbery Medal (*The Summer of the Swans,* 1971), the American Book Award (*The Night Swimmers,* 1981) and the Edgar Best Mystery (*Wanted… Mud Blossom,* 1992).

> **Facts and figures**
> *The Midnight Fox* was written in 1968 and first published in the UK in 1970 by Faber and Faber. It was published by Puffin in 1976. The latest edition was published by Faber and Faber in 2006. The book contains line illustrations by Martin Salisbury.

Guided reading

First reading

The first reading should be used to familiarise the children with the story and introduce the characters, events and key themes. Look together at the cover of *The Midnight Fox*. Ask the children what kind of novel they think this might be. (Scary, exciting, an adventure?) Ask them what they know about the author and if they have read any other books by her. Next, read the back-cover blurb and quotations. Ask what more we learn about the story from this. (The story is about a boy called Tom who reluctantly goes to stay on his aunt's farm in the summer holidays, and how there Tom sees a fox which he has to try and save from danger.) Query the title, eliciting that it carries two ideas: the idea of a fox glimpsed at midnight, and also a black fox, with fur as black as night.

Conflict

Read the first chapter with the children. Ask them to summarise the conflict between Tom and his parents. Why do they want him to go to the farm and why is he so against it? What do we learn about Tom from this opening chapter? (He likes model making, he is frightened of animals, he can't swim and so on.) What clues are there as to where the story is set? (The spelling of *Mom* and the price of the model in dollars tell us that it is set in the United States.) Read on to the end of Chapter 4. Ask the children what makes Tom so reluctant to go to the farm. (He thinks he will be expected to do hard chores, and also he will miss what is going on at home.) Who does Tom compare himself unfavourably to? (His capable, sporty Dad and also the athletic Bubba.)

Turning point

Read through Chapters 5 to 7. Summarise how Tom is feeling in his first days on the farm (really bored) and what is so exciting about the sighting of the fox. (It is unexpected, fleeting, a close/intimate encounter with a wild animal.)

Pause at the point where Hazeline tells her story to ask what has changed the complexion of the story: what implied threat is there? (That the fox will steal chickens and will have to be trapped or shot.) Continue through to the end of Chapter 10. Ask the children if they can summarise the feelings that Tom has towards the fox. (He admires and respects her, wants to protect her.) Pause at the end of Chapter 10 and identify the 'foreshadowing' that the author uses as a page-turner, making us wonder what terrible thing will happen.

Dilemma and resolution

Read through to the end of Chapter 15. Ask the children to explain Tom's dilemma. (He is torn between his family loyalties, given that Aunt Millie has lost her turkey and hen, but he can't bear the idea of the fox or her cub being killed.) Challenge them to explain the concept of *Tacooma*. What does this show about the way Tom is feeling? (He feels totally powerless as if he would need to invoke some magic power to stop Uncle Fred's plan.) Read on to the end of Chapter 17 and ask the children what fears Tom has to overcome to protect the foxes. (His fear of heights, climbing a tree, and also facing the wrath of his uncle.) Finish the story, pausing to ask the children how they think Tom feels now about his summer on the farm.

Second reading

The second reading provides an opportunity to identify some of the key themes of the story (friendship, self-esteem, the relationship between people and wild animals) and also to focus on language features (descriptive writing, use of simile and metaphor) and plot features – in particular how the author weaves together what happens in the present with the wanderings of Tom's mind, both to past memories and also into a world of imagination and fantasy.

Begin by focusing on the first two paragraphs and point out how the author begins with the highest and lowest point in Tom's encounters with the fox, using these as 'hooks' that encourage us to read on and find out what happened during *that summer* and on *that last terrible night*.

Narrative style

Continue reading to the end of Chapter 4 then ask the children if they can summarise what we learn about Tom (his hobbies, likes and dislikes, relationship with his parents and best friend Petie). What sort of man is Tom's father? (Sporty, masculine, always in control.) How is Tom different from him? (He is a worrier, sensitive, often feels out of control with his fears and emotions.) Consider the narrative style and ask the children how different the story might be if it were told in the third person. Point out how the first-person narrative allows us a diary-type insight into Tom's thoughts and feelings. Tom narrates events, but we also access his memories, imagination and fantasy. Cite some examples of this – such as his 'cowboy' fantasy of milking the cow and his memories of the Kewpie doll's head.

Read Chapter 5, pausing to ask the children whether any of them has had an experience they think similar to Tom's – something really awesome or unexpected. Why does he decide not to add it to his letter to Petie? (He feels it won't do it justice and Petie won't understand.) Discuss why Tom keeps the fox secret. (The sightings seem special and intimate and also he wants to protect her.)

Language and humour

Read on to the end of Chapter 10. Pause to highlight language or narrative features, for example, simile used to enrich descriptive detail of the fox or setting (*white-tipped tail as light as a plume; a hornets' nest like a huge grey shield*). Ask the children what part humour plays in the story and where we find it, for example in the light-hearted banter and play between Hazeline and Mikey, in Petie's newspaper headlines and questionnaires, and also in Tom's fantasies (such

as training cows to be dancers). Suggest that humour is important both to character and also plot, in that it shows us how Tom is gradually beginning to unwind and enjoy himself on the farm.

Ask the children how Tom's hotchpotch of memories, such as finding the marbles with Petie or seeing the sailing ship in the museum, relate to his sighting of the fox. (These are special moments that have stuck in his mind, representing something totally unexpected and lucky or just very beautiful and amazing.) Pause to highlight the 'foreshadowing' in the ominous words at the end of Chapter 10 and remind the children how the author used the same device as a 'hook' at the start of the novel.

Character and change

Read to the end of Chapter 15. Focus on the dilemma that faces Tom. Ask the children why they think he does not confide his feelings about the fox to Uncle Fred. (He is afraid they will not understand and be angry with him or think he is being stupid or disloyal as the fox has stolen his aunt's turkey and hen.) Touch on the fact that this ties in with Tom's characteristic insecurities – he worries that he is a disappointment to his parents and his uncle and aunt because he is not 'outdoorsy' and sporty like his Dad, Uncle Fred or Bubba.

Continue to the end of the story. Discuss what Tom has to overcome to protect the fox: his fears of climbing down the tree, and confessing what he has done to his uncle and aunt. What qualities do the children think this shows? (Bravery, courage, determination?)

Read to the end of the story. Discuss how differently Tom feels about the farm as he is leaving, from when he first arrived. Ask the children how they think he has changed and why. Challenge them to cite evidence from the text. Encourage the children to share times they have experienced where they were reluctant to go somewhere or do something, but were then really pleased that they had, because they enjoyed it and discovered new interests or friends.

Guided reading

Structure

At the end of the story, ask the children to look back at the contents page and consider the way the story is constructed in chapters. Can they identify any chapters that represent turning points in the story? (*The Black Fox*, *Tragedy Begins*, *The Stormy Rescue*.) Which parts did they find most exciting or enjoy most?

Encourage them to support their answers with reasons. Look again at the book cover and blurb. What kind of story do they think this is? (Realistic, a story that raises issues, an adventure?) Again encourage them to give their reasons. Tell the children that *The Midnight Fox* has been called a 'classic children's novel'. What qualities do they think it has that make it a 'classic'?

Shared reading

Extract 1

● Read an enlarged copy of Extract 1. Ask the children how Tom and his parents are feeling. (Tom is unhappy and resentful about having to go to the farm; his parents feel awkward and uncomfortable because they know he doesn't want to go.) Why does his Dad buy him the souvenirs? (To try to cheer him up.)

● Ask the children if any of them recognises the reference to the movie (a film of the novel *Anne of Green Gables* by the Canadian author LM Montgomery). What do Tom's thoughts tell us? (He thinks he will be a disappointment to his aunt and uncle because he is not muscular and sporty and good at outdoor work.)

● What clues to the setting can the children find in this extract? (The American spelling of *Mom*, words like *candy, north forty* and the reference to *all fifty states*.) What do the arrowheads in the souvenir shop tell us? (That they are near Native American country.)

Extract 2

● Read an enlarged copy of Extract 2. Ask the children how Tom is feeling at this point about staying on the farm. Encourage them to find evidence. (He talks about his *favourite place*; he feels relaxed enough to lie down on the rock, half asleep in the sun; he has become fascinated by the fox.)

● Encourage the children to think about the description of setting. Circle the words *ravine, boulders, foliage, underbrush*. Can they describe what sort of terrain this is (rocky, wooded)? Ask them to find a simile the author uses to evoke atmosphere (*tree trunks like fallen idols*).

● Next focus on the description of the fox, and again underline similes the author uses (*as easily as a cat, like a sail, black as coal*). Examine each one in turn, asking the children what qualities they convey (the ease of her movement, the full 'brush' of her tail, the colour of her fur).

● Discuss what Tom finds so exciting about these sightings (he is glimpsing into the world of a wild animal, a rare black fox) and how it is different from his usual favourite hobby, model making.

Extract 3

● Read an enlarged copy of Extract 3. Ask the children if they can explain what is happening and describe the mood. (Tense and anxious, because Uncle Fred is intending to shoot the fox.) Why do they think it seemed to get dark quickly that night? (Uncle Fred is waiting for dark when the fox will appear, and Tom is dreading this.)

● How does the author build a sense of tension? Encourage the children to cite evidence from the text. (The heat has been building, and now a storm is brewing; Uncle Fred sits absolutely still and silent, watching and waiting.) Discuss how the summer heat affects characters and plot more generally. (Aunt Millie gets irritable and insists the fox must go when it takes her turkey.)

● How do the children think Tom is feeling at this point? (Worried about the fox and her cub but powerless to stop what might happen.) Can they recall any other points in the story when there is heightened tension? (When Uncle Fred discovers the fox's den; when Tom goes out in the storm to rescue the fox cub.)

Extract 1

We left for the farm the next morning after breakfast. No one had much to say, so my mom turned on the radio and we listened to a disc jockey playing hit songs from the past. About noon we stopped for a picnic lunch by a place that advertised candy, fireworks, toys, real arrowheads, flags, coins, and souvenirs from all fifty states. I used to like to spend hours looking at that kind of stuff, but that day I didn't even feel like going inside. Finally, after we ate, my dad said, 'Come on, sport, I'll buy you something,' so we went in and I selected a little totem pole that had been made in Japan, and then he made me get this fake plastic ice cube which had a fake fly in it and we went out and put it in Mom's cup for a joke. It was a very dismal morning.

The rest of the way I just sat in the back seat with my eyes closed. I started thinking about a movie I saw once where some farm people sent to the orphanage for a boy, because they wanted someone to help with the hard work on the farm. Instead of the boy, the orphanage sent them a puny girl, and there was tremendous disappointment. I thought now that perhaps Aunt Millie and Uncle Fred were letting me come because they thought I was a great athlete with muscles like potatoes who could toss hay into the loft without spilling a straw. They would be very excited, of course, at the thought of this wonderful summer helper, and as our car drove up, they would be standing in the yard saying things like 'Now we have someone to break the wild horses for us,' and 'Now we have someone to get the boulders out of the north forty.' Then I would step out and they would cry, 'But where's the *big* boy?' and I would say, 'I'm the only boy there is.'

Text © 1968, Betsy Byars.

Extract 2

The days and weeks passed quickly, long warm days in which I walked through the woods looking for the black fox.

The next time I saw her was in the late afternoon at the ravine.

This was my favourite place in the forest. The sides of the ravine were heavy dark boulders with mosses and ferns growing between the rocks, and at the bottom were trunks of old dead trees. The trunks were like statues in some old jungle temple, idols that had fallen and broken and would soon be lost in the creeping foliage. There was only an occasional patch of sunlight.

At the top of the ravine was a flat ledge that stuck out over the rocks, and I was lying there on my stomach this particular afternoon. The rock was warm because the sun had been on it since noon and I was half asleep when suddenly I saw something move below me. It was the black fox. There was a certain lightness, a quickness that I could not miss.

She came over the rocks as easily as a cat. Her tail was very high and full, like a sail that was bearing her forward. Her fur was black as coal, and when she was in the shadows all I could see was the white tip of her tail.

As I watched, she moved with great ease over one of the fallen trees, ran up the other side of the ravine, and disappeared into the underbrush.

I stayed exactly where I was. My head was resting on my arms, and everything was so still I could hear the ticking of my watch. I wanted to sit up. I am sort of a bony person and after I have been lying on something hard for a long time, I get very uncomfortable. This afternoon, however, I did not move; I had the feeling that the fox was going to come back through the ravine and I did not want to miss seeing her.

Text © 1968, Betsy Byars.

Extract 3

It seemed to get dark quickly that night. Uncle Fred was already out on the back porch. He had brought out a chair and was sitting with his gun beside him, pointing to the floor. I never saw anyone sit any quieter. You wouldn't have noticed him at all he was so still.

I stood behind him inside the screen door. Through the screen I could see the tiny fox lift his black nose and cry again. Now, for the first time, there was an answer – the bark of his mother.

I looked towards the garden, because that's where the sound had come from, but Uncle Fred did not even turn his head. In a frenzy now that he had heard his mother, the baby fox moved about the cage, pulling at the wire and crying again and again.

Just then there was the sound of thunder from the west, a long rolling sound, and Aunt Millie came to the door beside me and said, 'Bless me, is that thunder?' She looked out at the sky. 'Was that thunder, Fred?'

'Could be,' he said without moving.

'Look!' Aunt Millie said, 'I swear I see black clouds. You see, Tom?'

'Yes'm.'

'And feel that breeze. Honestly, when you think you have reached absolutely the end of your endurance, then the breeze comes. I could not have drawn one more breath of hot air, and now we are going to have a storm.'

We stood in the doorway, feeling the breeze, forgetting for a moment the baby fox.

Then I saw Uncle Fred's gun rise ever so slightly in the direction of the fence behind the garage. I could not see any sign of the fox, but I knew that she must be there. Uncle Fred would not be wrong.

Text © 1968, Betsy Byars.

Plot, character and setting

Fox country

> **Objective:** To sustain engagement with longer texts, using different techniques to make the text come alive.
> **What you need:** Copies of *The Midnight Fox*, photocopiable page 15, individual whiteboards and pens, flipchart.
> **Cross-curricular links:** Geography, science.

What to do
● Tell the children that they are going to focus on the setting for the story, both in terms of the countryside or 'terrain' and the climate or weather. Read Chapter 10 together. Ask the children if they can pick out any specific features about the landscape that Tom describes, and list them on the flipchart (for example *rocks, ravine, boulders, creek*). Can they list any animals, other than the fox, that he describes? (For example *crayfish, chipmunks*.)
● Let the children work in pairs to scan the chapter for information about the setting. Prompt with questions such as: *What animals or insects does Tom see?* Ask the children to write down their findings on their whiteboards.
● Bring the class back together and list their suggestions on the flipchart. Then hand out copies of photocopiable page 15 and ask the children to fill them in, scanning the novel for information.
● Discuss the setting in the context of the story. Is it an important feature and if so how? (The fox's habitat, a rural experience for Tom, countryside issues such as culling foxes.)

> **Differentiation**
> **For older/more confident learners:** Invite children to draft a short description of the countryside around the farm.
> **For younger/less confident learners:** Let children draw a picture of the farm and the countryside around it, labelling key features.

Mapping the story

> **Objective:** To make notes on and use evidence from across a text to explain events or ideas.
> **What you need:** Copies of *The Midnight Fox*, a flipchart, writing materials and paper.
> **Cross-curricular link:** Geography.

What to do
● Tell the children they are going to focus on the description of the farm and note all the key features of the farm and the surrounding countryside. Read Chapter 5 together.
● Ask the children to summarise any particular features of the farm, using evidence from the text (for example the pond, the rope swing on the tree in the front yard). List their suggestions on the board. When they have scanned through the chapter, as a shared activity, extend the list on the board using evidence from the text about the wider countryside (the creek, ravine, stream and so on). They can refer to the notes they made on photocopiable page 15 in the previous activity.
● Ask the children to work in pairs to list any key events that happened at places listed on the flipchart. (For example, Tom spots the fox at the ravine, he rescues the cub from a rabbit hutch beside the garage.) When they have completed their lists, ask them to work together to draw a simple map showing the key features of the farm and surrounding countryside, and then label it with key events.

> **Differentiation**
> **For older/more confident learners:** Children could write a map key defining key terms such as ravine, pond, thicket.
> **For younger/less confident learners:** Provide a list of key events to label the map.

Plot, character and setting

Tom's thoughts

> **Objective:** To understand underlying themes, causes and points of view.
> **What you need:** Copies of *The Midnight Fox*, flipchart, photocopiable page 16.
> **Cross-curricular link:** ICT.

What to do

● Read Chapter 4 together. Ask the children to summarise what Bubba's room says about him and how Tom feels in comparison with him. (Bubba was a sporty boy, an outdoors type, had lots of skills and interests and Tom feels weak and puny compared to him.)
● Tell the children they are going to imagine the profile that Bubba might have on a social networking site when he was Tom's age. Arrange the children into pairs and give them time to plan out what they might include. Write some prompt questions on the flipchart: What sports does he practise? What are his hobbies? What does he collect? How would he describe his home life and family background?
● Bring the class back together and fill in their suggestions on the flipchart. Compare and contrast them with Tom's own likes and dislikes. Discuss how Tom imagines Bubba. (Sun-tanned, confident, muscular?) Remind the children how Tom feels he lets his father down with his lack of *control* and sporting prowess.
● Hand out photocopiable page 16 and ask the children to fill them in.

> **Differentiation**
> **For older/more confident learners:** Let the children use ICT skills to develop their social networking profile for Bubba.
> **For younger/less confident learners:** Children could draw a picture of Bubba's bedroom and add labels to the contents explaining what they tell us about him.

Past and present

> **Objective:** To understand how writers use different structures to create coherence and impact.
> **What you need:** Copies of *The Midnight Fox*, flipchart or board.

What to do

● Read Chapter 10 together. Point out that the narrative here is not just a straight recount of what happened at the ravine. Ask: *How do Tom's thoughts wander?* (Into memories of past or future events and into imagination or fantasy.)
● Ask the children if they can recall other examples from the novel of Tom's thoughts when they stray into past memories or go into fantasy. (For example his memory of the *Petie Burkis special* or his fantasy about finding a new colour.)
● Arrange the class into pairs and invite them to scan the novel to find examples of Tom's memories or imaginings. When they have finished, write two headings 'Memories' and 'Imagination' on the flipchart and write down their findings.
● Discuss how these contribute to the narrative. For example, his memory of finding the marbles helps explain the impact of the fox sighting as something unexpected and lucky; his memory of the movie about the puny girl arriving on a farm from an orphanage shows how he thinks his uncle and aunt will see him; the fantasies of dramatic news headlines are often funny and contribute to humour in the story.

> **Differentiation**
> **For older/more confident learners:** The pairs could try mapping out the plot showing different narrative elements (for example recount, memory, imagination).
> **For younger/less confident learners:** Children could try classifying their findings under headings: memories of movies, adventures with Petie, imaginary news reports and so on.

Plot, character and setting

Storyboard

> **Objective:** To explore how writers use language for comic and dramatic effects.
> **What you need:** Copies of *The Midnight Fox*, flipchart, individual whiteboards and pens, photocopiable page 17.
> **Cross-curricular links:** Art and design, drama.

What to do

● Read together Chapters 16 to 17 from *It seemed to get dark quickly that night*. Tell the children they are going to imagine that they are recording this episode for a film. Explain that films are often mapped out as a series of pictures – a storyboard. They are going to write notes to brief an illustrator for a storyboard relating Tom's rescue of the fox cub.

● Before they begin, as a shared activity, consider some dramatic effects that the author describes, for example, sound effects (the storm brewing, the shutters banging, the cry of the baby fox, the clatter of the dishpan) and tense scenes like Tom creeping downstairs or climbing down the tree. Write their ideas on the flipchart.

● In pairs, ask the children to make notes for the characters and props needed for their film. Then let them work together to make notes on the key scenes and dramatic effects.

● Hand out photocopiable page 17 and invite the children to complete them in pairs, writing a detailed brief for six main scenes from the film.

> **Differentiation**
> **For older/more confident learners:** Children can try storyboarding another episode from the story.
> **For younger/less confident learners:** Pairs could swap their storyboards and draw pictures from the briefs.

Headline news

> **Objective:** To explore how writers use language for comic and dramatic effects.
> **What you need:** Copies of *The Midnight Fox*, individual whiteboards and pens, photocopiable page 18.
> **Cross-curricular link:** Citizenship.

What to do

● Ask the children if there are any parts of the story that they found funny. Identify the main sources of humour – funny things that Petie says or does, the ups and downs of Hazeline and Mikey's relationship, and the dramatic newspaper headlines that Petie and Tom think up about things that happen in their lives.

● Discuss how humour contributes to characterisation, especially for characters like Petie and Hazeline. Write three headings on the board: 'Description', 'Dialogue' and 'Action' and challenge the children to find examples of each conveying the funny side of Petie's character. (For example, the description of Petie Burkis in the imaginary game show *'This is your bad moment'*; the dialogue about the corn and deodorant adverts; the episode where Petie puts the Kewpie doll's head on Tom's pillow.) Focus in particular on the news headlines that he creates and what makes them funny – how he dramatises mundane events as if they are disaster news stories.

● Hand out photocopiable page 18 and ask the children to fill them in.

> **Differentiation**
> **For older/more confident learners:** Children could try choosing more incidents from the story to write Petie-style news headlines about.
> **For younger/less confident learners:** Provide support by drafting a Petie-style headline for one of the incidents as a shared activity before the children complete the photocopiable sheets.

Plot, character and setting

Farm holiday

> **Objective:** To independently write and present a text with the reader and purpose in mind.
> **What you need:** Copies of *The Midnight Fox*, flipchart, farm-holiday brochures/advertisements (optional).
> **Cross-curricular links:** Art and design, ICT.

What to do

● Read Chapter 1 together. Discuss how Tom's parents try to 'sell' the stay at his uncle and aunt's farm to him (they tell him he can see baby lambs, collect fresh eggs, go swimming in the pond) and why Tom thinks he will hate it and is so reluctant to go (he is afraid of animals and thinks he will have to do chores).

● Tell the children they are going to imagine that they are writing a brochure to attract visitors to stay on the farm for a farm holiday. Refer to some examples of farm-holiday brochures in print or online if possible. The children need to think about all the things that might attract people to stay on the farm and in the surrounding countryside – for example, activities (fishing, hiking, swimming), the landscape (creeks, woods) and animals they can see (both on the farm and in the wild).

● Arrange the class into pairs and invite them to scan the novel for ideas. When they have finished, bring the class back together and write some of their suggestions on the flipchart.

● Let the pairs plan and design their brochures.

> **Differentiation**
> **For older/more confident learners:** Children could use ICT skills to develop their brochures.
> **For younger/less confident learners:** Children could use art and design skills to develop their brochures.

Best mates

> **Objective:** To understand underlying themes, causes and points of view.
> **What you need:** Copies of *The Midnight Fox*, flipchart, individual whiteboards and pens.
> **Cross-curricular link:** PSHE.

What to do

● Read Chapter 2. Ask the children to describe Tom and Petie's friendship – they hang out together, enjoy banter and laughs together, play tricks on each other and so on. Why do they think Tom enjoys spending time with Petie? (He makes him laugh with the things he gets up to and his crazy newspaper headlines.)

● Arrange the children in pairs and challenge them to write down some of the funny adventures with Petie that Tom recalls (the *Petie Burkis Special* recipe, the tricks they played with the Kewpie doll's head and so on). When they have finished, write their suggestions on the board.

● Challenge the pairs to imagine another adventure that Tom might have with Petie. Encourage them to think of something funny or crazy, or both. Prompt them with some starter ideas, for example, Petie might get into trouble trying to film the hornets' nest, or the boys might get into trouble with an experiment they do in science club.

● Bring the class back together and share some of their ideas. Discuss which are most convincing and why.

> **Differentiation**
> **For older/more confident learners:** The children can work in their pairs to draft Petie-style headlines and short news reports on their imaginary episodes.
> **For younger/less confident learners:** The children can discuss in pairs what makes best friends, and why Petie and Tom have a good friendship.

Plot, character and setting

Fox country

● Write down what you know about the countryside around the farm.

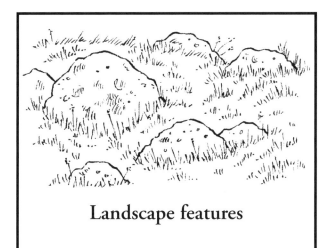

Landscape features

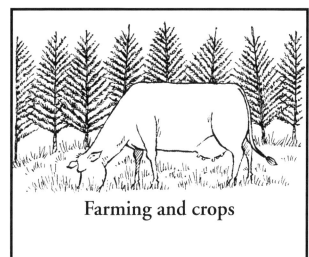

Farming and crops

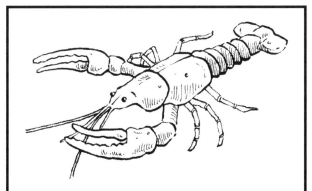

Animals and birds
you might see

Climate and weather

Illustration © 2010, Mike Phillips/Beehive Illustration.

Plot, character and setting

Tom's thoughts

● Describe what Tom thinks about the things in the speech bubbles and why he thinks this.

How others see him

Why?

Swimming

Why?

Animals

Why?

Bubba

Why?

Summer camp

Why?

Illustration © 1994, Martin Salisbury.

Plot, character and setting

Storyboard

● Write notes explaining what each scene in the storyboard should show. Include instructions for characters, setting and action. Add more boxes on the other side of the sheet if you need to.

Scene 1	Scene 2
Title: _____	Title: _____
Setting: _____	Setting: _____
Characters: _____	Characters: _____
_____	_____
Action: _____	Action: _____
_____	_____
Scene 3	**Scene 4**
Title: _____	Title: _____
Setting: _____	Setting: _____
Characters: _____	Characters: _____
_____	_____
Action: _____	Action: _____
_____	_____
Scene 5	**Scene 6**
Title: _____	Title: _____
Setting: _____	Setting: _____
Characters: _____	Characters: _____
_____	_____
Action: _____	Action: _____
_____	_____

■ SCHOLASTIC
www.scholastic.co.uk

PHOTOCOPIABLE

READ & RESPOND: Activities based on The Midnight Fox

Plot, character and setting

Headline news

● Explain the events behind these imaginary headlines.

Cow attacks boy – scientists baffled

Boys drowns – girl photographs it

Farm girl's eyes produce record -breaking eight hours of tears

● Write headlines for the newspaper stories about:

The 'Petie Burkis Special'

Tom's rescue of the fox cub

Tom and Petie's time capsule

READ & RESPOND: Activities based on The Midnight Fox

Illustration © 2010, Mike Phillips/Beehive Illustration.

■SCHOLASTIC
www.scholastic.co.uk

Talk about it

Feelings

> **Objective:** To use the techniques of dialogic talk to explore ideas, topics or issues.
> **What you need:** Copies of *The Midnight Fox*, flipchart, individual whiteboards and pens, photocopiable page 22.
> **Cross-curricular link:** PSHE.

What to do

● Read at pace the first two chapters. Ask the children to summarise what the argument between Tom and his parents is about.

● Arrange the children into groups and ask them to list in two columns all the reasons why Tom's parents want him to go to the farm and all the reasons he doesn't want to go. Encourage them to think about the things Tom will miss as well as what he thinks he will dislike about the farm, and why Tom's parents believe it will benefit him, as well as allowing them to have their holiday.

● Bring the class back together and discuss whether Tom should go, asking the children to support their answers with reasons. What should his parents say to persuade him? Encourage the children to relate to their own experiences of trying something new.

● Hand out photocopiable page 22. Ask the children to work with a talk partner to discuss the questions about Tom's feelings and then complete the sheet.

> **Differentiation**
> **For older/more confident learners:** Children could try composing an email to Tom, persuading him why he should go to stay on the farm.
> **For younger/less confident learners:** Ask children to discuss in their groups similar experiences they have had, and why sometimes it is good to break out of your 'comfort zone'.

New surroundings

> **Objective:** To reflect on how working in role helps to explore complex issues.
> **What you need:** Copies of *The Midnight Fox*, flipchart or board.
> **Cross-curricular links:** Drama, PSHE.

What to do

● Read together Chapter 3 up to *honked the horn all the way to the highway*. Ask the children how Tom is feeling at this point (sad and abandoned). How do they think his parents are feeling (a bit worried about him, maybe slightly guilty)?

● Discuss briefly why Tom is feeling so reluctant to stay on the farm, and how he is different from his cousins, Fred and Millie's sons. Jot down some of the children's ideas on the flipchart.

● Arrange the class into groups of four. Tell them that they are going to improvise a short drama playing the roles of Millie and Fred and Tom's

mum and dad. They should imagine what Tom's mum and dad might say to Millie and Fred about their son when he is out of the room (what sort of boy he is, why he is feeling a bit nervous). They should think what Millie and Fred might say to reassure them everything will be all right.

● Allow them time to practise and then invite groups to perform for the class. Invite constructive feedback.

> **Differentiation**
> **For older/more confident learners:** Let children improvise another scene between the four at the end of the holidays.
> **For younger/less confident learners:** Discuss in detail how Tom feels about the farm and why his parents might worry, and what Millie and Fred might say about their own boys and why Tom will have fun there.

Talk about it

Imagine that!

> **Objective:** To improvise using a range of drama strategies and conventions to explore themes such as hopes, fears and desires.
> **What you need:** Copies of *The Midnight Fox*, flipchart, photocopiable page 23.
> **Cross-curricular link:** Drama.

What to do
● Read together Tom's fantasy about discovering a new colour from the beginning of Chapter 7. Check that the children understand the reference to *colour television*, and explain that in the 1970s, when the novel was published, colour television was only just coming in; up until then people had watched black and white sets.
● Arrange the class into small groups and tell them they are going to improvise the television report in which Tom appears with his discovery. They can decide on other interviewees who might appear, for example a geologist might identify the mineral that Tom has dug up or someone might talk about the retail potential of using a new colour in manufacturing. They should decide who will play Tom, the presenter and any other characters in their scene. Give the children photocopiable page 23 to help them plan their ideas or to use as a prompt sheet.
● Allow them time to plan and improvise their scenes, then invite groups to perform in front of the class. Encourage constructive feedback on the content and presentation.

> **Differentiation**
> **For older/more confident learners:** Children could plan and improvise another scene based on the boys' idea '*This is your bad moment*'.
> **For younger/less confident learners:** Provide them with support in preparing for their scenes, such as questions the presenter could ask Tommy (what, how, where, why, when).

Time capsule

> **Objective:** To use the techniques of dialogic talk to explore ideas, topics or issues.
> **What you need:** Copies of *The Midnight Fox*, flipchart, individual whiteboards and pens.
> **Cross-curricular link:** History.

What to do
● Read the last chapter of the novel. Focus on the time capsule that Tom and Petie bury. Discuss the things they put inside to tell future generations about their lives. Ask: *Which might be most interesting or revealing and why?*
● Ask the children what they might put in a time capsule about their lives. Discuss what types of things would be most revealing to future generations. What would they most like to find in a time capsule buried by someone their age, 100 years or 1000 years ago?
● Arrange the class into pairs. Tell them they are going to plan what Tom might put into a time capsule to remind himself of his time on the farm. They could include photographs, drawings, words, and 'found objects' like a leaf, stone or feather. They should scan the novel for ideas.
● Bring the class back together and write some of their ideas on the board. Let the class choose six of the best ideas for the time capsule, giving reasons for their choices.

> **Differentiation**
> **For older/more confident learners:** Ask children to write down what they would put in their own time capsule, listing six objects they would include with their reasons.
> **For younger/less confident learners:** Let children draw some objects they would put into a time capsule about their own life, with labels explaining what they are and why they have included them.

Talk about it

Awesome!

Objective: To explore how writers use language for comic and dramatic effects.
What you need: Copies of *The Midnight Fox*, flipchart, photocopiable page 24.

What to do

● Tell the children to close their eyes while you read aloud Chapter 5, from *There was a very nice place over the hill* to the end of the chapter. Ask the children what they see in their imagination and what makes the sighting of the fox vivid. Write the headings 'Appearance' and 'Actions' on the flipchart and ask the children what details they can recall about the fox, listing their suggestions under the appropriate heading.
● Arrange the class into pairs and challenge the children to find similes that describe the fox's appearance and actions. When they have finished, review their findings and discuss how the author uses similes to heighten descriptive detail. Elicit the qualities that are conveyed: lightness, agility and so on.
● Hand out photocopiable page 24 and ask the pairs to discuss the prompts together.
● Bring the class back together and discuss what makes the fox sightings so *awesome* to Tom – they are fleeting, unexpected, outside his control, he has never seen a fox in the wild, a black fox is rare.

Differentiation
For older/more confident learners: Children could scan the novel for more examples of descriptive similes.
For younger/less confident learners: Provide page references to help children discuss the prompts on the photocopiable sheet.

The hunting debate

Objective: To present a spoken argument, sequencing points logically, defending views with evidence and making use of persuasive language.
What you need: Copies of *The Midnight Fox*, flipchart, individual whiteboards and pens.
Cross-curricular links: Drama, science.

What to do

● Tell the children that they are going to focus on the dilemma that Tom faces when he discovers Uncle Fred is intent on killing the fox.
● Briefly discuss the two points of view: why Aunt Millie is upset and why Tom wants to save the fox.
● Arrange the class into small groups. Ask them to discuss all the reasons that are raised in the novel for killing or not killing the fox. They should make two columns on their whiteboards to record all the arguments on each side. Encourage them to think of persuasive arguments on both sides, modelling examples. For example: 'Farmers have the right to protect their stock' or 'Wild animals have the right to live their lives'.
● Bring the class back together and share their findings, using two columns on the flipchart to record the arguments on either side.
● Discuss the type of persuasive language that could be used for both points of view.
● Broaden the arguments into a class debate on the fox-hunting issue. Encourage the children to express personal views, supporting their arguments with reasons.

Differentiation
For older/more confident learners: Let the groups script a short dialogue in which Tom tries to persuade Uncle Fred not to kill the fox.
For younger/less confident learners: Let the groups discuss what Tom could say to persuade Uncle Fred not to kill the fox.

Talk about it

Feelings

● Talk to your partner about the following questions then write down your ideas on the sheet.

Tom's nose runs when he is upset. Think of two occasions when this happens and explain why.

1.

2.

Describe an occasion when Tom is happy on the farm.	Think of and describe an occasion when Tom is unhappy on the farm.
Describe an episode from the past when Tom felt happy.	Describe an episode from the past when Tom felt unhappy.

Talk about it

Imagine that!

● Use this sheet to help you create a television report about Tom's discovery of a new colour.

BOY UNEARTHS BRAND NEW COLOUR

Illustration © 2010, Mike Phillips/Beehive Illustration.

Talk about it

Awesome!

● Discuss why the sighting of the fox reminds Tom of the following things.

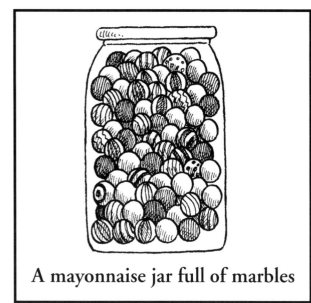

A mayonnaise jar full of marbles

An old model of a sailing ship

Playing Monopoly

An old newspaper

Illustration © 2010, Mike Phillips/Beehive Illustration.

SCHOLASTIC
www.scholastic.co.uk

READ & RESPOND: Activities based on *The Midnight Fox*

Get writing

Tom's diary

Objective: To use a range of narrative devices to involve the reader.
What you need: Copies of *The Midnight Fox*, flipchart, photocopiable page 28.

What to do

● Read Chapters 14–17 together. Point out that these chapters record a single, eventful day on the farm. Tell the children they are going to plan a diary entry that Tom might write, recording the events of the day. Explain that they will need to decide what to include and what to leave out, as the diary entry will need to be a concise summary of what happens.

● As a shared activity, work through the text, making notes on the flipchart that record key facts or events – the hot weather, the tense mood, pumping water from the pond, the fox hunt, the cub as bait, Uncle Fred's watch, the rescue of the cub, Tom's admission.

● Arrange the class into pairs and hand out photocopiable page 28. Ask the children to fill in the diary planner, scanning the text for information and using the flipchart notes to help them.

Differentiation
For older/more confident learners: Challenge the children to choose another day to record on the diary planner.
For younger/less confident learners: Provide support for the children in extracting key facts or events by highlighting relevant text.

Fox poems

Objective: To select words and language drawing on their knowledge of literary features and formal and informal writing.
What you need: Copies of *The Midnight Fox*, flipchart, examples of concrete/shape poems (optional), writing materials and paper.
Cross-curricular link: Art and design.

What to do

● Read Chapter 10 together. Tell the children they are going to focus on the words and phrases that the author uses to describe the fox. Pick out one or two relevant phrases and write them on the board as examples.

● Arrange the class into pairs and ask them to scan through the chapter writing down all the relevant words and phrases. They should include descriptions of her appearance and also how she moves and reacts. Allow them time to scan the rest of the novel for more words and phrases describing the fox.

● When they have finished, bring the class back together and list some of their suggestions on the flipchart, discussing which they think are most vivid and have most impact.

● Challenge the pairs to think up some more phrases or words that they would use to describe the fox, adding these to the word bank.

● Tell the children they are going to write a short poem about the fox, choosing words or phrases from the word bank. If they want, they can experiment with a shape or concrete poem, using the shape of the animal or its head.

● Allow the children time to write their poems then share some with the class, inviting constructive feedback.

Differentiation
For older/more confident learners: Pairs can work as response partners to help children edit and improve their poems.
For younger/less confident learners: Model a simple poem before children begin drafting.

Get writing

A letter to Petie

> **Objective:** To use different narrative techniques to engage and entertain the reader.
> **What you need:** Copies of *The Midnight Fox*, flipchart, writing materials and pens.

What to do

● Read Chapter 5 as far as *I wrote a long letter to Petie.* Tell the children they are going to plan and write the letter that Tom might have written.

● Ask the children to prepare by reading Chapters 3 and 4 which describe Tom's journey and arrival at the farm and his first few days there. When they have finished reading, discuss as a class things he might want to tell Petie – for example, what the journey was like, how he felt when they arrived, what his bedroom is like and how he has been spending his time. Write their suggestions on the flipchart.

● Allow the children time to plan and draft their letter. Before they begin, encourage them to think of anything Tom might want to ask Petie, based on what he was going to miss – for example, he might want to ask Petie about the hornets' nest, or what he has been watching on television. Briefly recap on letter form (they should include a date and address for the farm).

● When they have finished, bring the class back together and invite volunteers to read their letters. Encourage constructive feedback and criticism.

> **Differentiation**
> **For older/more confident learners:** Children could draft some emails or text messages that Tom might send Petie from the farm.
> **For younger/less confident learners:** Children could work with a writing partner to compose their letter.

Fox-spotter guide

> **Objective:** To adapt non-narrative forms and styles to write fiction or factual texts.
> **What you need:** Copies of *The Midnight Fox*, flipchart, photocopiable page 29, access to the internet.
> **Cross-curricular link:** Science.

What to do

● Tell the children they are going to focus on facts that we learn about the fox from the novel, and then do some more research on foxes so they can write an entry for a wildlife-spotter guide.

● Arrange the class into small groups and ask them to scan the novel for any facts that Tom learns by watching the fox, or is told by others (for example Uncle Fred or Hazeline). Remind them they are not looking for *description* of the fox now, but *facts* – for example, the fox has a den and hunts mice and other small animals.

● Bring the class back together and list their facts on the flipchart.

● Provide internet access and tell the groups they are going to research some more facts on foxes. Prompt them with key areas to research such as size and appearance, habitat and diet. They could also look for some facts about rarer black foxes.

● Hand out photocopiable page 29 and ask the children to complete the spotter guide, using information from the flipchart and their own research.

> **Differentiation**
> **For older/more confident learners:** Let children use the information to draft a short non-chronological report about black foxes.
> **For younger/less confident learners:** Provide children with a list of questions to help them with research, for example, 'What do foxes eat?'

Get writing

Questionnaire

> **Objective:** To adapt non-narrative forms and styles to write fiction or factual texts.
> **What you need:** Copies of *The Midnight Fox*, flipchart, examples of magazine questionnaires (optional), writing materials and paper.
> **Cross-curricular link:** PSHE.

What to do

● Read Chapter 9 from *We went in and Aunt Millie said, 'Tom, there's a letter for you...'* to *She always liked everyone to give full attention to their eating.*

● Ask the children if they have come across multiple-choice questionnaires like this in comics or magazines. Provide examples if possible. Tell the children that psychologists use similar tests to reveal personality traits, for example, when someone is applying for a job.

● Arrange the class into small groups. Tell them that they are going to devise six questions for a questionnaire that Tom might send back to Petie. Explain that it should be based on things Tom sees or thinks about on the farm. Before they begin, ask for some ideas for possible topics and write them on the flipchart: Bubba, Tom's farm chores, his idea for the cow circus, the old flying man and so on.

● Allow the groups time to devise and write their questionnaires, then encourage them to exchange them with other groups and fill in their answers. Share some of the funniest or most imaginative ideas with the class.

> **Differentiation**
> **For older/more confident learners:** Let the groups devise a multiple-choice questionnaire about the novel.
> **For younger/less confident learners:** The groups can invent more Petie-style questions about their own lives.

Book review

> **Objective:** To write reflectively about a text.
> **What you need:** Copies of *The Midnight Fox*, flipchart, photocopiable page 30.

What to do

● Explain to the children that they are going to plan a review of *The Midnight Fox*, incorporating information about the plot, setting and characters, as well as practical information on the author.

● Look together at the cover and illustrations in the book. Ask: *What sort of mood or atmosphere do they capture?* (Magical, exciting, dangerous?) *What elements of plot do they convey?* (Tom anxiously watching the fox, his Uncle with the gun, the stormy night when Tom rescues the cub.) Read the blurb and ask the children to recap on the 'hook' that makes us want to read the book: to find out whether and how Tom rescues the fox.

● Divide the class into small groups. Encourage the children to discuss their favourite parts of the story and any aspects of plot, setting or character that they like or dislike.

● Hand out photocopiable page 30 and ask the children to use their ideas to fill it in, as a planning sheet for a book review.

● The groups can discuss their ideas and explain the reasons behind their choices.

> **Differentiation**
> **For older/more confident learners:** Let children use the internet to find out more about the author and add information on her and her other novels to their notes, then write up their reviews.
> **For younger/less confident learners:** Ask children to write up their book review.

Get writing

Tom's diary

● Plan a page of Tom's diary, using the class notes and the book to help you.

An extraordinary day!

What the weather was like

_____

How everyone was feeling

_____

What I did in the morning

_____

What happened:

1. On the fox hunt

_____

2. When we brought the fox cub back

_____

3. After dark

_____

How I feel tonight

_____

Illustration © 2010, Mike Phillips/Beehive Illustration.

Fox-spotter guide

● Use your research notes to create a fox-spotter guide.

Red Fox

Latin name/family: _____

Size and appearance: _____

Habitat: _____

Diet: _____

Behaviour (breeding/hunting): _____

_____

Characteristics (vision/smell/call): _____

_____

Variant (black fox): _____

Interesting facts: _____

_____

_____

_____

Illustration © 2010, Mike Phillips/Beehive Illustration.

Get writing

Book review

- Use this page to plan out your review of *The Midnight Fox.*

The Midnight Fox

Author:

Illustrator:

Choose two words that you think describe the story and explain why.

exciting   **funny**   **sad**   **tense**

Choose two words that describe Tom's character and explain how.

brave   **sensitive**   **clever**   **kind**

Choose your favourite part of the story and explain why you like it.

Write down the two main themes in the novel.

1.

2.

PHOTOCOPIABLE

PAGE 30

SCHOLASTIC
www.scholastic.co.uk
READ & RESPOND: Activities based on *The Midnight Fox*

Assessment

Assessment advice

Assessment should be an ongoing process, allowing children and teachers to consolidate progress and work on areas that require improvement. In *Read & Respond: The Midnight Fox*, the children are asked to complete a range of activities to develop their speaking, listening, reading and writing skills. It is important to explain the objective of the activity clearly at the beginning of each lesson and, if possible, relate it to other literacy work or relevant subjects in the curriculum. At the end of lessons, children should be encouraged to assess their own work against the objectives set, and decide how successful they were and which areas need improvement. For many tasks they will work with a writing partner or in small groups and they should be encouraged to work collaboratively and offer constructive criticism on each other's work. Teachers can assess progress on written work and also on classroom observation of individual, paired and group work. The assessment activity on photocopiable page 32 can be used to assess the children's grasp of underlying themes in the novel.

Themes and features

> **Assessment focus:** To deduce, infer or interpret information, events or ideas from texts.
> **What you need:** Photocopiable page 32, flipchart or board, individual whiteboards and pens.

What to do
● Discuss together the main events and themes in *The Midnight Fox*. Ask the children to give their subjective opinions of the story and to support their views with reasons. Ask them if it has encouraged them to read other work by Betsy Byars and, if so, why? Which aspects of her writing style did they enjoy? (For example, bits that made them laugh, vivid description, Tom's far-fetched imaginings.) Encourage them to cite examples from the text.
● Discuss how different the novel would be if it were written in the third person. Suggest that getting inside Tom's head and understanding how he is feeling is crucial to the development of the book's key themes.

● Focus on Tom's character and ask the children if they found him likeable and believable. As a shared activity, construct a mind map for Tom, writing down the children's ideas on the board. Write Tom's name in the centre, then draw radiating lines to boxes containing key facts about him, for example, he can't swim, he is scared of animals, his nose runs when he gets upset. Encourage the children to use evidence from the text to support each statement. Discuss how, in creating Tom's character, the author balances his shortcomings (nervousness, lack of athleticism) with qualities like kindness, sensitivity and bravery. The children could go on to extend the mind map with further details, working on individual whiteboards or paper.
● Ask the children to work on their own to complete photocopiable page 32, using their knowledge of *The Midnight Fox*. Encourage them to refer back to the story as closely as possible for examples.

Assessment

SECTION

7

Themes and features

● Explain how these themes feature in *The Midnight Fox*.

Friendship	The natural world

Self-esteem and overcoming fears	Countryside issues

● Getting inside Tom's head is crucial to our understanding of the book. Can you find one or more examples of each of the following?

Tom's observations

Tom's memories

Tom's imaginings

Tom's stay on the farm changes him because…

READ & RESPOND: Activities based on The Midnight Fox